DEPLOYED FLIGHT AND SOMETIMES ETERNITY

Other Books by Ronnie Smith

The Last White Ruby

The Royal Princess and the Three Magical Gifts

Roses for the Most High:
Poetry Celebrating the Mystical Christian Path

The Sky is for Wonder

DEPLOYED
FLIGHT
AND
SOMETIMES
ETERNITY

RONNIE SMITH

COLONEL, USAF RETIRED

PLENUS GRATIA PUBLICATIONS®
SAINT LOUIS, MISSOURI

Copyright © 2020 by Ronnie Smith | www.PlenusGratia.com

All rights reserved. No part of this publication may be reproduced, distributed or transmitted, in any form, or by any means, including photocopying, recording, or other electronic or mechanical methods, without the prior written permission of the publisher, except in the case of brief quotations embodied in critical reviews and certain other noncommercial uses permitted by copyright law. For permission requests, write to the publisher, addressed "Attention: Permissions Coordinator," at the address below.

Ronnie Smith/Plenus Gratia Publications®
Saint Louis, MO 63109
www.PlenusGratia.com

The appearance of U.S. Department of Defense (DoD) visual information does not imply or constitute DoD endorsement.

Cover and Interior Design by The Book Cover Whisperer: ProfessionalBookCoverDesign.com

Back Cover Photo Courtesy Colonel Mark Doll, USAF, Retired

Deployed Flight and Sometimes Eternity/Ronnie Smith. —2nd ed.

ISBN 978-0-9980465-4-9

Printed in the U.S.A.

SECOND EDITION

*This book is dedicated to the memory of
Lieutenant Colonel John MarcWolfgang . . .
Patriot, Airman, Father, Grandfather,
Husband, Wingman*

Contents

INTRODUCTION i

BATTLE YOU WON 3

SNAKE DANCE IN THE SOMALI FAMINE 7

TO VENUS AND COOK 9

MOBILITY AIR 11

THE ART OF AIR WAR 15

CHANT TO THE C-130 19

THE AIRCRAFT BONEYARD 23

THE SARAJEVO AIRLIFT 27

MISSION TO SOTO CANO AIR BASE 29

THE PANAMA ROTATION 33

POLAR AVIATORS 37

MISSION TO THE POLAR PLATEAU (AGO 4) 41

REFUELING BYRD STATION, ANTARCTICA 45

ICEBREAKER PICNIC 47

THE LAST NAVIGATOR 49

WHITE HARP 55

THE POLAR ROAD 59

RETURN OF THE POLAR SEA 63

WINTER FLIGHT OVER ARCTIC NORWAY 67

BIPOLAR 69

THE GREAT LEAP 71

NINE ONE ONE	75
DEPLOYED SALUTE	77
DREAM TO FLY	79
AUTHOR'S NOTE	83

List of Figures

Photo by Author, U. S. Navy S-3 Viking Sub-Hunter, Courtesy of the 309th Aerospace Maintenance and Regeneration Group (AMARG), Tucson, Arizona 5

C-130 Hercules Tail Flashes on the Parking Ramp, Photo courtesy Brig Gen Ed Vaughan, USAF 13

USAF FB-111 Formation, Public Domain, Courtesy USAF, Credit Camera Operator: Msgt. Buster Kellum 17

USAF C-130 Hercules Landing on Dirt Strip, Photo, Public Domain, credit courtesy of USAF 21

Photo by Author, Courtesy of the 309th AMARG, Tucson, Arizona 25

Photo by Author, Courtesy of the 309th AMARG, Tucson, Arizona 31

AC-130 Spectre Gunship, Photo Public Domain, Courtesy of United States Air Force 35

LC-130 Hercules Ski-Bird Skiway Takeoff, Photo by Colonel Mark Doll, USAF (Retired), Courtesy of United States Antarctic Program 39

LC-130 Ski-Bird Takeoff, McMurdo Station, Antarctica, Photo by Colonel Mark Doll, USAF (Retired), Courtesy of United States Antarctic Program 43

Parking Coordinates & Tail Number at B-52 Navigator Station, Photo by Author; Courtesy of the 309TH AMARG, Tucson, Arizona 53

Photo by Colonel Mark Doll, USAF, Retired, Observation Hill, Antarctica, Courtesy of United States Antarctic Program 57

Near Hut Point, McMurdo Station, Antarctica, Photo by Colonel Mark Doll, USAF (Retired), Courtesy of United States Antarctic Program 61

US Coast Guard Polar Sea about to dock at McMurdo Station Ice Dock, Photo Public Domain, Courtesy United States Antarctic Program 65

LC-130 Ski-Bird Ramp, McMurdo Station, Antarctica, Photo by Colonel Mark Doll, USAF (Retired), Courtesy of United States Antarctic Program 73

USAF T-37 Tweet, Undergraduate Pilot and Navigator Trainer, Photo courtesy of the 309th AMARG, Tucson, Arizona.................................... 81

Introduction

THE MILITARY FORCES of the United States execute a program of flying that exceeds the scope of any other nation. It is very dynamic all told, and its success depends on a number of exterior pillars of support. The civilian defense sector combines with the organic maintenance, logistics, and support branches of each service, to help the operators execute the mission of a diverse U.S. capability. That said, it was extremely gratifying to serve and fly with our allies and friends of foreign services many, many times.

After flying for roughly 25 years in the Air Force from a number of different bases and flying wings, I wanted to capture a tiny fraction of the inspirational experiences. There were often subtle miracles, and sometimes dog days, which eventually led to contentment of a completed task. What was that life like in toto? It spanned a large part of the globe, all seven continents, in the only aircraft I flew, the C-130 Hercules. That turned out to be a blessing for a navigator in a wartime, peacetime, and polar mission. It was like a marriage. I loved it and it was challenging. Many of these poems can be seen as snapshots into the mission-life of this sector of the Air Force.

The journey of military men and women starts with an oath. My particular road started in a Cold War. 1982. Sometimes wars that weren't official wars. These played out in Central America, in the early days of Bosnia, and later when units deployed supporting the drug cartel interdictions. We Americans served at home and abroad in the desert wars of Southwest Asia and Afghanistan. We served humanitarian relief across the Balkans, Africa, and many other places. We airlifted hurricane relief to our domestic and foreign Caribbean shores. And we resupplied across both polar icecaps. This book spans a dynamic time and tries to explain some of the experiences that weighed and played out on that sometimes mundane, sometimes exotic stage of the world.

I wish to offer special thanks and indebtedness to Brigadier General Ed Vaughan, USAF and Colonel Mark Doll, USAF (Retired) for their vital input and pictorial contributions during the making of this book. It was an honor to have served alongside them.

Battle You Won

By standing to battle you won

Before the acclaim and the sorrow
The strike of the arrow of passion
Had rainmakers spilling bombs away

That damned every battle you won

You targeted foes like El Zorro
Their strongholds you left were left ashen
In crosshairs that filled and marked that day

And branded the battle you won

You hammered horizon's war-glow
That zippers of guns would fashion
And streak the black hills that bark dismay

Expanding the battle you won

With parachutes airborne with ammo
Our warriors would plummet to mash-in
The drop zones and drill the darkened clay

And landing in battle you won

That shield with the steel of the morrow
From faith of a bountiful ration
A blazing bastille to the stark and gray

That standing to battle you won

Photo by Author, U. S. Navy S-3 Viking Sub-Hunter, Courtesy of the 309th Aerospace Maintenance and Regeneration Group (AMARG), Tucson, Arizona

IN 1992, THE UNITED NATIONS confirmed the emergency of Somalia's oncoming famine that would starve 4.5 million people as a result of seasonal dry conditions concurrent with civil war via military coup that took place in Somalia. Held in truce by warlords, Somalia opened its doors to the U.S. Operation Provide Relief, which was quickly morphed into Operation Restore Hope (1992-1994) by US Forces under a Unified Task Force. The UN was incapable of establishing such an operation that the military is perfectly equipped to do. Dirt airstrips around the country were reconned by U.S. Army Special Forces personnel, U.S. Marines were deployed, and Air Force combat control teams set up and controlled the airfields for C-130 operations into and out of the country each day from nearby Kenya. There were no forklifts or other mechanized lifts at these dirt airstrips. Offloading the tons of grain sacks were done one by one, by the sweat of men's backs. These sometimes became culturally intimate encounters

Snake Dance in the Somali Famine

Somali desert, its listless mile
swept by cobras and camels
hill country clans plodding single
file across blood-baked clay
an ant-army from our altitude
to a refuge by a dirt airstrip
starvation's canvas of desolation

Your famine and genocide invoked
this beast of burden
with a belly of steel and engines
that scatter every creature
pallets of grain piled like ant hills
black skinned men toting bags
on their backs

Dripping their mosaic of sweat, an
art on bodies that rags cannot cloak
Humility shines in ebony pillars
when they relax to lean between lifts
To the weary, clapping revives rhythms
of dance, connecting to hands
of a thousand generations
Parched toes, the texture of earth
thump the jumping dust
shaking the saints from the tree of life
no slaves in the heart of the savior.

CAPTAIN JAMES COOK, Royal Navy, in the late 1700s circumnavigated the globe twice and mapped numerous islands and coastlines in the New World and the Pacific Ocean theretofore unseen by European explorers. On his first voyage around the globe the British Admiralty at the request of The Royal Society tasked him with the scientific mission of tracking Venus in its transit across the Sun via sextant measurements from the Pacific Ocean. This, the great navigator did. This information ultimately contributed to the ability to measure the distance from the Earth to the Sun.

To Venus and Cook

Perhaps the greatest captain known was Cook
Who sailed around the globe beyond all lands
As continents would cast their longing look
They navigated straits for other sands

Who sailed around the globe beyond all lands?
Chronometers would clock the very deep
They navigated straits for other sands
To check the transit Venus had to keep

Chronometers would clock the very deep
Antarctic shores were but the lore of time
They checked the transit Venus had to keep
Across a sun afar from Britain's rime

Antarctic shores were but the lore of time
Imagined by the weight that worlds disperse
Across a sun afar from Britain's rime
The veil of Venus glides the universe

Imagining the weight that worlds disperse
I levitated through a sextant's eye
On veil of Venus rode the universe
And summoned dreams I never questioned why

I watched her travel through a sextant's eye
And sought the greatest captain known as Cook
Who captured dreams that answered every why
As continents would cast their longing look

Mobility Air

Ripples through earth snap the fleet to the air
Strapped in the seat before sunrise, the door
   of morning threw gruel to an aircrew
   Who train to hone their weapon of wings
     to fly and to fight, evacuate tears
from a world turned underside up, a shore

   that lost its balance with land, ever sure
with cries through the crazed and violent air
  And rowdy, we shall fly and fight in tiers
    aloft, to re-tank from a gas-bank door
  There's dance and death in a ballet of wings
   on missions at night for unsung aircrew

  For to fly and fight—the right of aircrew
  when holocaust lacerates home and shore
  They land in dirt in the blow-storm of wings
    offload and exert in engine-blast air
to erase the dearth; push wealth from the door
    of a combat bird of ten volunteers

  And tankers will race to a war that tears
   the land and foists the voyage of aircrew
For they stack with their back to fear; endure
   the urgent storm and the aerial shore
    We fly and fight for corridors of air
   heaving machines of levitating wings

Tendons of Hercules buttress the wings
wrought by the sweat that bought the budgeteers
The airborne steer and leave rifts in the air
where parachutes streak to drop-zones. Aircrew
will fight to fly and glide on to the shore
when nobody knows, a lance through the door

of terror, for many keep shut the door
and fear; and fears that are un-slain are wings
without mercy—mobility brings shore
through the clouds of dust and muck's profiteers
Who wrestle reward from lords and aircrew
Who throttle despair through turbulent air

Because columns of air shall lift the door
to fly and fight as aircrew; gauging their wings
on all frontiers, whatever danger ashore

C-130 Hercules Tail Flashes on the Parking Ramp
Photo courtesy Brig Gen Ed Vaughan, USAF

The Art of Air War

Sculpted to fight, to incite
the battle floor and chaos restore
to an enemy with no political remedy
From factory mill to sweat's will
you peel the eye of the sun; fight begun
in your rivet sprayed titanium maid
whose white-hot hose bellows
cymbals of American steel; We'll
fly stars washed in blue—fear the view!
Rat-tat-tat spat by a gray bat
with radar and a roar

*USAF FB-111 Formation, Public Domain, Courtesy USAF,
Credit Camera Operator: Msgt. Buster Kellum*

Chant to the C-130

Propellers chop a gut-sung choir
A lot of hop from stubby form
On shattered fields that bind the world
Where wings of valor glide the wind

With airborne pluck through gun-lit fire
A daisy cutters' tropic storm
Through shattered fields that bind the world
Where wings of valor glide the wind

Our jacked-up trips through drug empire
Narcotic jungle's greed would swarm
These shattered fields still bind the world
And wings of valor glide the wind

Yet Sarajevo won't expire
That siege of years became the norm
For shattered fields that bind the world
The wings of valor glide the wind

The paratrooper's taut steel wire
Will bring it (!) and let strength transform
Those shattered fields that bind the world
Where wings of valor glide the wind

In desert dust when hope was dire
Our mission was—We must perform!
Through shattered fields that bind the world
Still wings of valor glide the wind

USAF C-130 Hercules Landing on Dirt Strip
Photo, Public Domain, credit courtesy of USAF

THERE ARE A NUMBER of aircraft boneyards. The largest, the 309th Aerospace Maintenance and Regeneration Group (309th AMARG), is often called 'The Boneyard', located in Arizona. The 309th AMARG is sole repository of out-of-service aircraft from all branches of the US government. The arid climate of the region makes it an ideal location for storing aircraft.

The Aircraft Boneyard

You entered the silent life
to respire with desert
A churchyard of warcraft
Some, whose gallant returned
to reside in the sanctuary of deeds
Regrets of sad crusade by candle
of distant lightning
Like the ghost in this gravestone
whose engines echo
drumming hummingbirds
that etch the epitaph

We strain through windowpanes
nailed shut by the past
From the days you trained
like this sun that vaults the desert
—without fail—
to catapult your fierce heart
whose bloodshot eyes widened
to jack a fire-scream dream
upon the hell of the world

Photo by Author, Courtesy of the 309th AMARG, Tucson, Arizona

OPERATION PROVIDE Promise was a humanitarian relief operation in Bosnia and Herzegovina during the Yugoslav Wars, from 2 July 1992 to 9 January 1996, which made it the longest running humanitarian airlift in history. Sarajevo was one of many hubs in the region where Allied Forces resupplied its people under the UN combat operation.

The Sarajevo Airlift

We wanted to save you
O hopeless Sarajevo

Hollowed tenements
skeletons of your war bride
Snipers on hills
greeting your genocide
Airdropped supplies
tumbling your countryside
Firestorm nights
hatred they deified

The prayer that we gave you
O hopeless Sarajevo

IN THE 1980S, Soto Cano was a newly ramped up air base in Honduras, with freshly milled wood huts for aircrew rest and training of the Honduran military ongoing. There was one place to eat and drink, and it was an austere tour of one year for ground personnel. The taxiways and ramps were still red clay. We tried to bring back fresh milk whenever we'd return there.

Mission to Soto Cano Air Base

There was more than the tropics to face
but then we were the ones getting paid
in a jungle that choked an air base
in a flight suit that sweat overplayed

And the corps built a club for a hub
and the huts for our hooches in shade
And our plane masked terrain that could rub
from the radar the shadows we sprayed

Didn't mind the political pools
We dropped dimes in the canyons and laid
on a cutout dirt strip with some tools
and saw critters that stalked unafraid

If one sortie, it seemed like a few!
But a tub full of ice would cascade
as we swam to the bottom for brew
to clear out the red dust of our trade

Photo by Author, Courtesy of the 309th AMARG, Tucson, Arizona

THE PANAMA ROTE known as Volant Oak, was an ongoing C-130 operation out of Howard Air Base, Panama, assisting local allies and serving the U.S. Embassies throughout Central and South America.

The Panama Rotation

On a route around Cuba
We flew through invisible alleys
Parading no neighbor to find you
At the isthmus where hemispheres weld

We dropped our ramp on that tropical world
Somewhere there was a regime in charge
Arriving with original American gifts
The things that made us gringos

Through your windows to nowhere's ville
Seeming to me, never-been-there-ville
I wrote of you in letters that lay incomplete
Your torn canopy opened to mystery

Yielding a spyhole to the Latino masses
The fragile people who get swept away
By politics, bullies, landslides and hurricanes
Migrating across the headlines of nations

Your virgin rainforest, prostituted canal
Your polychrome birds, bright dark-eyed people
Your black beaches and Incan temples
Tap mountain lakes, motionless in rarefied air

We'd leave you like the lost colony of Roanoke
Often saying we'd return with good tidings
A yearning, but not what we learned from life
Because princes always said to leave you alone

AC-130 Spectre Gunship
Photo Public Domain, Courtesy of United States Air Force

IN THE POLAR REGIONS, one danger is that of crevasses covered by snow, called snow bridges, which can be so deep, one cannot see the bottom. Antarctica is also known for its archaeological finds of dinosaurs and fossilized plant life. 450 million years ago the continent was located in the mid-latitudes as part of a great land mass that split up into the continents we have today.

Polar Aviators

A snow dome entombs
the time of reptiles
mausoleum where scaly
skulls rampage through
rock and monster old earth
In their reddened sunbed
slain, a stampede stopped
atop the bottom
of the world for the
white-away of beastdom

For aviators to ski
through slippery clouds
flipped upside down
plated from pale to gray
intimate textures to aviators
define this dry rainbow

To be ever wary of shadowed
crevasses cloaked in snow
Of jaws that resurrect T. Rex
swallowing the light

That airmen might slide
their turbo-ride
across an edifice of ice
and transform it into sky

LC-130 Hercules Ski-Bird Skiway Takeoff
Photo by Colonel Mark Doll, USAF (Retired)
Courtesy of United States Antarctic Program

SEVERAL AUTOMATIC GEOPHYSICAL Observatories (AGOs) are located on the polar plateau in Antarctica, where the barometric pressure can push the altitude above 12,000 feet above sea level routinely. Several hours of flight are required to get to the sites to maintain these platforms. They gather data to understand the high latitude atmosphere of Earth interacting with the magnetosphere and solar wind from our Sun, the origin of high energetic forces producing Earth's aurora activity and other space weather phenomena. Thin air, high altitude, and absence of wind are challenges to take off in ski-equipped LC-130 aircraft.

Mission to the Polar Plateau (AGO 4)

We strapped on the Herc
to ping pong ball space
for what might remain
or nature erase

Yet on the plateau
two miles above sea
the air is so shallow
that breathing ain't free

Upon this white comet
with nothing else near
a socket and grommet
will strain 'til they tear

And gunned by the pain
of cold's bitter grip
our loadmasters drain
by steam of our ship

The sons of John Wayne
would survive the thin air
and surged like a train
through sweat and the wear

To fail on this stage
the prize of the day
we squeezed every gauge—
no fun and no play!

And packed in that can
where vapors perfumed
we cracked out a plan
for takeoff that loomed

We tried every fix
to gain on the snow
and sighed when that mix
gave one slide to go

With blast of our rockets
and pilot's finesse
some tricks in his pockets
our ticket, I guess

We never gave in
on high plains of snow
the ice will not win
where breeze will not blow

LC-130 Ski-Bird Takeoff, McMurdo Station, Antarctica
Photo by Colonel Mark Doll, USAF (Retired)
Courtesy of United States Antarctic Program

Refueling Byrd Station, Antarctica

A flight
a floating tableland
a below into nowhere
of a fuel atoll of
nowhere gnomes
Where the sun
is a spinning top
round the pole
Its glitter-dust spraying
fairyland frozen air

Because water
cannot weep here
not even heat can seep
into the rare light, lost in the

silence of the drone of engines
silence in the blare of infinite blue

Humans remain mute
like astronauts
passing in space
buoyant across the
omni-white
using sign-language protocol
in this particular no-place

Fuel grimed overcoats
lurch upright, unhook the aircraft
sullied snowmen out of place
disturbing nowhere

Icebreaker Picnic

Long whiles awake
you make a lake
and pile ice cake

And then First Mate
assessed the plate
and mulled the fate

Create sea lanes
allow whale trains
to swim these plains

For penguin play
a-flap the fray
will soon mayday

A boatswain's stake
will park, partake
with sliding brake

At dock so slick
the frozen stick
you've stuck to tuck
at polar picnic

The Last Navigator

Jacket slung to the bunk
data dancing in the head
A mission's must-haves of

Checklists
Time hack
compasses
pencils
ring laser gyros
Omega
LORAN
GPS
radio altimeter
radar altimeter
latitudes
longitudes
plotters
dividers
sextant
rhumb line
coriolis
precession
nutation
cheat sheets
air almanac
star charts
H.O. 249 sight reduction tables
groundspeed

Indicated Airspeed
True Airspeed (TAS)
TAS check
knots
drift
dead reckoning-DR
pressure
lines of position
air plot
fuel log
flight log
forms
category one
whiz wheel
magnetic variation
gauges
gauge error
true heading
GRID
Grivation
compass corrections
Greenwich hour angle
sidereal hour angle
local hour angle
ZN-zenith
azimuth
Transverse Mercator
Global Navigation Chart
polar projection
Operational Navigation Chart
fix
Jet Navigation Chart

civil twilight
Tactical Pilotage Chart
IFR approaches
Joint Operations Graphics chart
Airborne Radar Approaches
missed approaches
box pattern
lead-in flags
heading shots
airdrops
computed air release point
green light
red light
point of impact
HARP
night vision goggles
emergency egress
RADAR
flashlight
SCNS/Self-contained navigation system
Estimated Time of Arrival
waypoints
flight plan
Iridium phone
IFF Mode 4 transponder
KIK-18

must strap me in
with faith for flight
flying to execute
Art.

*Parking Coordinates & Tail Number at B-52 Navigator Station
Photo by Author; Courtesy of the 309th AMARG, Tucson, Arizona*

White Harp

Paradise made a white harp of the world
Pole unto Pole strings the arc of cold ages
Rippling meridians flown and then hurled
Ice-warped and wild as we plucked them like sages

Scientists count the uncountable snow
Higher and higher with melting in stages
Glaciers once bound only strain and let go
Savage the wave as the virgin one rages

*Photo by Colonel Mark Doll, USAF, Retired, Observation Hill, Antarctica
Courtesy of United States Antarctic Program*

The Polar Road

Perhaps this solo road
colors me like a whiteout
like an icecap over oasis
that puts to rest my dreams

As if I had an eye-patch
where you disappear
Where you, beneath this snow-place
won't be ubiquitous anymore

Near Hut Point, McMurdo Station, Antarctica
Photo by Colonel Mark Doll, USAF (Retired)
Courtesy of United States Antarctic Program

POLAR SEA IS THE U.S. Coast Guard Polar Class Icebreaker. The icebreaker mission in Antarctica for Operation Deep Freeze was to annually clear a navigable sea lane for the Military Sealift Command cargo and tanker ships to offload their supplies at the dock of McMurdo Station. The dock was a floating frozen block of ice, maintained each year.

Return of the Polar Sea

You toss arctic waves
and turn south, aweigh
to drone the torrid zone
slap the belly-belt
of the globe and sail
to southernmost fields
that bloom only ice
to bludgeon you

You too through the
shrapnel of floes
punish and tear
or veer to pioneer
as pancake ice re-rises
gripping with Antarctic
grit, sated and grateful
to greet you again

US Coast Guard Polar Sea about to dock at McMurdo Station Ice Dock
Photo Public Domain, Courtesy United States Antarctic Program

Winter Flight over Arctic Norway

Fjord wonderblue was never before
making white lake a big pale whale
hoarding fumes from fir-sweet floor

Fjord wonderblue was never before
naked white winter, angels nail
Nordic cross to anchor shore

Fjord wonderblue was never before
raking white gulls who shriek and wail
toward the sea to ever soar

AFTER 11 YEARS OF Petitioning, in 1982 Lynne Cox, an American swimmer, who held numerous open water records, received permission from Mikhail Gorbachev, then General-Secretary of the Soviet Union, to swim from the United States across the Bering Strait.

DATING BACK DECADES during the Cold War, the United States as part of NORAD installed and manned radar site stations across the rim of the North American Arctic and Greenland. This was called the Defense Early Warning system or DEW Line. Resupplying the DEW Line stations was the task of the L/C-130.

Bipolar

We peered North and South
as longitude lines lit a fuse at the poles
The two hinterlands are lockers
of one infinity
that hibernates deep cold

Early explorers took on
frozen
madcap
heroic
fragile
final excursions
pelted by everything
that can fall from heaven

Through despot ideology
we now drank its white lightning
for a Frankenstein-static high
We couldn't shrink from Cold War
We knew who was red or white

Our radars queued like penguins
peeking across the whitecap of the world
O, we charged our barbed wire sky
until the justice of one woman bridged
the Bering Strait in a bathing suit
That was 1982

Now warming seas surge both hinterlands
A schizophrenia, mostly manmade
If only we knew who we were
If only we cared who we were
And suicide was not an option

The Great Leap

El Teniente, dig to measure tombs of cold
For only eyes that shiver stow the ice age blight
of plains of snows and shadows. You'll declare, once here
to serve as servant, tyrant, czar—then hallowed stare
at floating diamond dust dispersing radiant light

El Teniente, you shall rattle jails of cold
You'll see the whitish blue of studded frozen belts
whose hailstone shards bejewel the wastes of priceless world
Its solid ocean, born of sudden death that swirled
the continents and poured to scour the mountains' welts

El Teniente, wastelands rail their ancient cold
Their lonely maelstrom came and slowed these sleds unkept
These broken holy yokes are not for minds so meek
They stomached murder of the herd that death would wreak
its ruthless truth for us, a summit some have leapt

El Teniente, scrolls of ice were slowly rolled
Untainted wisdom leaks where glacial fields unfold

*El Teniente, (el ten-en´-tay) Lieutenant, Hispanic

LC-130 Ski-Bird Ramp, McMurdo Station, Antarctica
Photo by Colonel Mark Doll, USAF (Retired),
Courtesy of United States Antarctic Program

Nine One One

We could not sing a song about towered inferno
And a bristling anthem would seal the new grave
From the core of the nation to desert saguaro
The unthinkable woke sleeping suckling and knave
Our undrinkable cup we must swallow and brave

Though the memory's distant, those days reappear
turning sadness and anger to patriot's glare
And our flags, they came flying, the things to count dear
With the smoke still arising that stained everywhere
With the smoke on horizon from guns that we'd wear

In the halls of the doctors of war there was might
But no antidote yet resurrects those who fall
In the house of the wounded there's plenty of fight
To avenge and expunge and relocate the brawl
To avenge the immediate, we'll make the call

In the vigils we carried a torch for the slain
On October the 7th we flew without fear
We sent message by B-52 and its train
And the hellions from warships to make it all clear
And by hellions of warships the tip of the spear

Deployed Salute

Years disappear
loosed like wild mustangs
never to tame
and this same daybreak
whose rising is a rite
unbridled by the freedom
of beauty to blaze back
the gate of day

perishes in the palm
of one last salute
affixed to the brow
warrior to arch of triumph

where I walked with
those fear-defiant
to reach and right
the anguish of the world
to stand with them
on solemn stone
a shield and sword with an oath
that raised this path to honor
and cleared the horizon
for eagles aflame

Dream to Fly

You sought the Air Force life, which longing sent
for you, young loves, to labor foreign lands
And bore me there; the zest of youth was spent
to bear the fruit of love that love commands

You taught my limbs, my mind, my heart, my hands
To kneel to God, engage the storied race
you let me run the laureled fields where stands
a test and price in living love's embrace

To claim athletic crowns, you let me chase
without a world awaiting grownup games
For dreams of burning passion won't erase
Nor melt the heart of fight that ever flames

When clouds, like fleeting seasons, seemed so high
To comb those clouds I leapt and dreamed to fly

*In dedication to SFC James Gordon and
Airman Barbara Ann Trhlik Smith, my parents*

*USAF T-37 Tweet, Undergraduate Pilot and Navigator Trainer
Photo courtesy of the 309th AMARG, Tucson, Arizona*

Author's Note

RONNIE SMITH grew up in Chicago, Illinois and Baltimore, Maryland. He earned a bachelor's degree at Loyola University Maryland, and later studied engineering at the University of Maryland. Colonel Ron Smith, retired from the Air Force after 30 years of service, where he commanded or flew over 1,000 flights in Antarctica. Challenged by extreme winds and temperatures that could drop to minus -75 degrees Fahrenheit during austral summer, physical and mental endurance were paramount to combat the rigors of prolonged operational stress. He discovered in that world contemplation and divine majesty. His poetry and paintings rest upon the foundation of the underlying wonder of God in humanity and creation. He continues to travel, write, and research the lives of the saints, mystics, and the religious cultures of his poetic subjects.

IF YOU HAVE ENJOYED reading this book, please post a review, long or short, on any book distributor sites (Amazon, Barnes and Noble, etc.). It is very appreciated and helps promote the work.

IF YOU WOULD LIKE to place a bulk order for your parish, school, or friends, then please note that we offer special discounts on quantity purchases made by corporations, associations, schools, and others. For details or any comments, contact the author at:

Ronnie Smith/Plenus Gratia Publications
PlenusGratiaToday@gmail.com
www.PlenusGratia.com

www.ingramcontent.com/pod-product-compliance
Lightning Source LLC
Chambersburg PA
CBHW041504010526
44118CB00001B/14